Ill Health

Ill Health

Wendy Bray

Text copyright © Wendy Bray 2005
The author asserts the moral right
to be identified as the author of this work

Published by
The Bible Reading Fellowship
15 The Chambers
Abingdon, OX14 3FE
United Kingdom
Tel: +44 (0)1865 319700
Email: enquiries@brf.org.uk
Website: www.brf.org.uk
BRF is a Registered Charity

ISBN 978 0 85746 231 2
First published 2005
This edition 2015
All rights reserved

Acknowledgements
Unless otherwise stated, scripture quotations are taken from the Holy Bible, New International
Version, copyright © 1973, 1978, 1984 by International Bible Society, are used by permission of
Hodder & Stoughton Publishers, a division of Hodder Headline Ltd. All rights reserved. 'NIV' is a
registered trademark of International Bible Society. UK trademark number 1448790.

Scripture quotations from The Revised Standard Version of the Bible, copyright © 1946, 1952, 1971
by the Division of Christian Education of the National Council of the Churches of Christ in the
United States of America. Used by permission. All rights reserved.

p. 14: Quotation from Jane Grayshon, *Treasures of Darkness*, Hodder and Stoughton, 1996, p. 9.
p. 17: Quotation from Hilary McDowell, *Some Day I'm Going to Fly*, Triangle, 1995, p. 3.
p. 22: Quotation from Alister McGrath, *Why Does God Allow Suffering?*, Hodder & Stoughton, 1992, p. 32.
p. 25: Quotation from James Jones, *People of the Blessing*, BRF, 1998, p. 155.
p. 28: Quotation from Wendy Bray, *In the Palm of God's Hand*, BRF, 2000, p. 36.

Cover photograph: © STOCK4B-RF/Gettyimages

Every effort has been made to trace and contact copyright owners for material used in this resource.
We apologise for any inadvertent omissions or errors, and would ask those concerned to contact us
so that full acknowledgement can be made in the future.

A catalogue record for this book is available from the British Library

Printed in the UK by Rainbow Print

Introduction

In 2004 I sat down to write a short booklet of Bible readings and reflections which might encourage and support those struggling with a period of ill health. I had recently completed a long round of treatment for cancer, and, unbeknown to me, was about to face the diagnosis of a second. What I couldn't have anticipated, and wouldn't have wanted to, was that eight years later I would be third time unlucky. At the very least, three encounters with cancer have given me some experience of that lonely, bewildering, life-changing place that is serious illness.

Each time I have found myself in that place, yet again, I have found it helpful to try to look beyond the illness, the symptoms, the hospital procedures and waiting times, and look instead to God. But that is often easier said than done, and being a smiling martyr in the face of suffering is nothing but damaging to us and unhelpful to those who love and care for us. What is needed is honesty—before God, one another and in the dialogue we so often have with ourselves.

God understands the gut-wrenching turmoil that often fills the 'waiting' times of those who are ill.

He is big enough to take our anger, confusion and doubt. He doesn't only take those things but helps us to embrace them, so that our relationships, our prayer and our attitudes might remain authentic, expressing 'where we are at' in a healthy way while maintaining resilience and retaining hope.

These readings are designed to help us find that authenticity—spiritual, emotional and relational—during a period of illness. They are intended to help us frame questions, even those of the almost impossible kind, and to hear God in response to those questions even when that response seems framed by the perplexing mystery of silence. They do not avoid asking us to face our emotions, our prognosis, or the practical issues we may have to tackle. Rather, they approach those anxieties from what might be a divine perspective, as far as that can be understood, as well as a human one. The hope they carry is that we will meet God in our fragile humanity in the midst of the most trivial and the most traumatic moments of illness and know his reassurance, even his blessing.

Our attention span is often short when we are ill, and reading may be tiring, so each reflection is designed to be easily 'paused' midway. Weekend readings are of a more contemplative, restful style and each concludes with a short prayer or reflection which can be returned to during the day or in the middle of the night. Some key topics, weakness for example, appear in several places with varying approaches so that connections can be made and remade between the word of God and the nitty-gritty of our experience.

Many of the verses and thoughts I have shared are drawn from my own reading, reflection and prayer and from diaries I kept over several years of illness. No two experiences of illness are ever identical, but I am grateful for the benefit I've received from reading the thoughts and understanding of those who have 'been there, had that' before me. Somehow sharing experiences, however traumatic, helps us feel less alone.

It is my prayer that this short book will make a real difference during difficult times by turning our hearts and minds to God, who cares for us in every detail of our experience of illness... and at this very moment... more than we can possibly know.

2 CORINTHIANS 4:16–18

Hidden futures

Therefore we do not lose heart. Though outwardly we are wasting away, yet inwardly we are being renewed day by day. For our light and momentary troubles are achieving for us an eternal glory that far outweighs them all. So we fix our eyes not on what is seen, but on what is unseen. For what is seen is temporary, but what is unseen is eternal.

Is it any wonder that our bodies don't always do their job properly, and generally wear out? They are just a temporary arrangement, not designed to last for ever.

Paul appreciates that we find our mortality depressing. He knows what it is to battle with illness, but reminds us that it is the unseen, in us and in eternity, that ultimately matters—not what we see and experience now.

Maybe Paul had his tongue fixed firmly in his cheek when he referred to 'light and momentary troubles'! Perhaps his perspective was such because he was able to contrast those 'light' troubles with a heavenly glory so great that it far outweighs them all.

Losing heart is easy to do when we're confined to home or hospital. Days are long and it often seems as if the rest of the world is going forward without us. We feel helpless and dark moods or tearfulness can catch us unawares.

Paul encourages us not to lose heart. 'Don't look at your circumstances,' he is effectively saying. 'Look heavenward... and keep on looking heavenward!'

If we can learn to look above illness and uncertainty, we might find, like Paul, that our situation is illuminated by the glorious reality we have yet to experience.

G.K. Chesterton said that 'heaven is peace dancing'. What a wonderful picture!

Tuesday

PSALM 121:5–8

Someone to watch over me

The Lord watches over you—the Lord is your shade at your right hand; the sun will not harm you by day, nor the moon by night. The Lord will keep you from all harm—he will watch over your life; the Lord will watch over your coming and going both now and for evermore.

The psalmist shows that God is the source of his ultimate protection—ultimate, because there are instances when our foot may slip. So does the psalmist have false hopes? No, he has faith. A slipping foot does not result in a loss of faith but a moment of doubt, and God's love and grace still surround that moment. We do not lose his protection, even if it may take an act of will to remember that.

Think of a mother watching her playing children from a distance. She must not stand over them or they will never learn to turn to her for help. They can run to her for assurance, or do without her comfort. Whatever their choice, though, she is always watching over them. This psalm reminds us of God's watchfulness, day and night. Nothing can happen outside his view. He watches us now and 'for evermore' (v. 8), into eternity.

If you are in hospital, you may know the feeling of lying awake at night in what seems to be a ward empty of nurses but full of other patients able to sleep when you can't. No one else may be watching us, but God our guardian is. He doesn't take turns to sleep like the nurses. He is ever watchful, ever wakeful.

During the day, wards and corridors are full of 'comings and goings'. Patients wait for doctors to arrive. Visitors and trolleys come and go. But the psalmist says that the Lord will even watch over our coming and going. He doesn't miss a thing.

In all 'comings and goings', remind me, Lord, that you watch over me.

JAMES 5:14–16a

A question of healing

Is any one of you sick? He should call the elders of the church to pray over him and anoint him with oil in the name of the Lord. And the prayer offered in faith will make the sick person well; the Lord will raise him up. If he has sinned, he will be forgiven. Therefore confess your sins to each other and pray for each other so that you may be healed.

God's healing includes both the medical and the miraculous. Whenever we hope for healing, it is important that God, not the illness, is the focus. We should always come to him in honesty and confession first, and pray for healing second.

If I'm not healed, does it mean I haven't enough faith? No! Jesus said that we only need a mustard seed of faith (Matthew 17:20). Healing does not depend on faith alone. We know only that God can heal—not that he will.

Paul, referring to some faithful biblical personalities, writes, 'These were all commended for their faith, yet none of them received what had been promised. God had planned something better' (Hebrews 11:39–40a). Trust God's perspective on illness and healing. He may have planned 'something better'.

When I was first diagnosed, I didn't go straight to my church leaders for anointing and prayer. I wanted to listen to God first. When I did ask them to pray for me, it was with a much clearer perspective on what God might be doing in my life. That view helped others to understand that it was God, not instant healing, that mattered. If I had been healed immediately, God would not have been able to touch literally thousands of lives through my diary (published 18 months into treatment).

God deals with each of us differently. That's why hearing *(God) rather than* healing *(me) should be the priority.*

Thursday

PHILIPPIANS 4:4–7

Pray first

Rejoice in the Lord always. I will say it again: Rejoice! Let your gentleness be evident to all. The Lord is near. Do not be anxious about anything, but in everything, by prayer and petition, with thanksgiving, present your requests to God. And the peace of God, which transcends all understanding, will guard your hearts and your minds in Christ Jesus.

Rejoicing isn't the first thing we feel like doing when we are unwell, but Paul's instruction is clear: 'Rejoice... always'. It is important enough to repeat (v. 4).

We're not asked to 'count our blessings' or scour around for something to be grateful for, but to shift our focus from our circumstances on to God. That may be more an act of will than desire, but a changed focus reveals a clear picture of God's faithfulness that produces heartfelt rejoicing—even if it is expressed by a wiggle of our toes under the bedclothes rather than a dance of joy. Our rejoicing reminds us that the Lord is near, that we need not worry about anything because we really can pray about 'everything'. As we trust him, we will know a peace so wonderful that it is beyond understanding.

One night, when I was very ill, I could not get from the bathroom back to my bed without help. Knowing that there is power in the name of Jesus, I began to whisper his name with what little strength I had. I began to experience an almost breathtaking peace. It was as if I was being lifted from that terrible weakness for just a few minutes. That peace that 'transcends all understanding' (v. 7) gave me the strength to reach my bed—and enjoy a rare peaceful night's sleep.

We need to remember Paul's order of things: rejoice, know God is near, pray with thanksgiving, and then know his peace as a practical reality.

Friday

2 CORINTHIANS 12:9–10

Strengthening grace

But he said to me, 'My grace is sufficient for you, for my power is made perfect in weakness.' Therefore I will boast all the more gladly about my weaknesses, so that Christ's power may rest on me. That is why, for Christ's sake, I delight in weaknesses, in insults, in hardships, in persecutions, in difficulties. For when I am weak, then I am strong.

Boasting about weaknesses isn't exactly in step with our power-hungry society. We are more likely to try to hide our weaknesses, or blame somebody else for them.

In these verses Paul links weakness with power—an unlikely alliance. What makes that alliance work is that the power he refers to is God's. It is a power beyond our comprehension, worked out according to very different rules of engagement for very different ends. This otherworldly power is available to us in times of weakness because we *don't* deserve it, not because we do. That's the essence of grace. It is given not because of who we are, but because of who God is—a God of grace, undeserved mercy and love. It is grace alone that transforms our weaknesses, but for his ends, not ours.

We all have days of tearfulness, doubt and worry, when we have no strength to persevere and feel like giving up. I suggest that you do just that: give it up—but give it up to God. Acknowledge that your weakness leaves your human power insufficient in the circumstances, but that God's power is sufficient.

God often asks us to remain weak just a little longer so that his strength can be best used in our circumstances. His power, not ours, is made perfect in the midst of our weakness.

Instead of feeling weak and wanting to be strong again, boast a bit, and let God transform your circumstances.

PSALM 84:5–7

Puddles and pilgrimage

Blessed are those whose strength is in you, who have set their hearts on pilgrimage. As they pass through the Valley of Baca, they make it a place of springs; the autumn rains also cover it with pools. They go from strength to strength, till each appears before God in Zion.

We are familiar with the analogy of life as a journey. What we tend to resist is the likelihood that our journey might take us along a less than easy road.

Illness, or a stay in hospital, may steer us unwillingly through what we see as a backwater, even a wilderness, where we are left feeling exposed to delay and frustration at best, and pain and suffering at worst.

As Christians, however, every twist and turn of our life's journey leads us heavenward. Like the pilgrims in these verses, we are headed for home, where we will worship God with our whole being and live with him as his children in the place prepared for us.

The psalmist tells us that these pilgrims do not have an easy journey, and neither will we. But God provides strength for the weak and refreshment for the thirsty. He gives blessings like 'pools' and the certain hope of meeting him at journey's end.

The valley mentioned here would remain arid without God's leading and blessing. The faith of the pilgrims and God's response turn it into somewhere strangely beautiful.

God knows that in the midst of our experience of illness we will often feel exposed, tired, weak and uncertain, but he will not let us go long without wiping the dust from our feet, bearing us in his arms and quenching our thirst with his love and blessing.

Ask God to give you a pool in which to paddle!

MATTHEW 11:28–30

Where to go for rest

'Come to me, all you who are weary and burdened, and I will give you rest. Take my yoke upon you and learn from me, for I am gentle and humble in heart, and you will find rest for your souls. For my yoke is easy and my burden is light.'

These verses are so familiar that it is easy to dismiss them as too idealistic amid the grim realities of illness. But if we look again, we discover a helpful pattern. Jesus offers rest when we are weary and burdened. To know it, we must first go to him, even in our weakness, to demonstrate our recognition of him as the source of that rest.

The rest he offers is not flopping down in mindless exhaustion. It is the result of a special partnership—an apprenticeship. Yokes are often designed for two to work together, as well as for one in submission. Jesus is offering us both mentoring and authority as we follow him, in order to achieve true rest that is everlasting, whatever our circumstances.

Jesus offers us rest for our souls, not necessarily our bodies. Does that mean that if we are in hospital, we will toss and turn again tonight, or find it difficult to sleep because of the pain, but that our 'soul' will be sleeping like a baby? Is he showing an interest only in what we call our 'spiritual' lives?

I don't think so. I believe that Jesus offers a spiritual rest which, when we have learnt it, underpins every part of our life—even the pain—and transforms long nights and doubt-filled days. Sometimes that might lead to less pain or fear. At other times we will still face trauma but know for certain that he bears the burden with us.

Daily remind me that you share this burden, Lord.

Tuesday

ROMANS 5:3–5

Disappointment

Not only so, but we also rejoice in our sufferings, because we know that suffering produces perseverance; perseverance, character; and character, hope. And hope does not disappoint us, because God has poured out his love into our hearts by the Holy Spirit, whom he has given us.

At first glance, these are not easy words. Pain and suffering are not something for us to rejoice in. Neither does God rejoice in them. It is what comes out of them that we often can rejoice in.

Paul says that one difficult step leads to another on a path of suffering, but we are not alone. Jane Grayshon—a nurse and writer who herself struggled with painful illness—wrote, 'When we do not find him in the rescue where we hoped him to be, he is in the very darkness itself.'

God shares the darkness, often silently, giving us the hope we need to carry on. Hope, far from being a weak, passive emotion, can be motivating. It can carry us along, empowered.

Disappointment is an inevitable feature of illness. We miss important events, feel that we are letting people down, or find ourselves unable to do things that really matter to us. Test results bewilder us, we fail to make the progress we had hoped for, or discover that a prognosis is suddenly worse. Friends may promise to visit or help out in some way, but they let us down. We may wait all day for the words, 'You can go home', but not hear them. Our hopes are dashed and disappointment settles like a cloud.

But that's human hope, not the hope that God offers. Our hope in God never disappoints because it is assured. He has promised that our hope in him will be fulfilled, and God always keeps his promises.

Lord, help me to keep you in sight amid clouds of disappointment.

ISAIAH 46:3–4

All my life

Listen to me, O house of Jacob, all you who remain of the house of Israel, you whom I have upheld since you were conceived, and have carried since your birth. Even to your old age and grey hairs I am he, I am he who will sustain you. I have made you and I will carry you; I will sustain you and I will rescue you.

These words fly in the face of our society, which says that only the young matter.

God makes a special point of mentioning that he has not forgotten those in the evening of their lives. In this case he is talking about his loving relationship with a whole nation, but he shows this same loving faithfulness to each one of us.

He is with us through every one of our days from conception to old age, and beyond. His hand never leaves our lives.

Notice that God's role is an active one. He doesn't just sit back and watch us meander our way through the years, but promises to reach out to uphold us, sustain us and rescue us. Every one of us will have known times when we have asked God to do one or all of those things. Like little children lifting their arms to a parent, God wants us to depend on him as Father God and recognise—perhaps today—our need to be carried.

Some time ago, I spoke at a retreat at which I encouraged a group of women, many in and beyond their 70s, to look back over their lives and reflect on the ways that God had sustained, carried and rescued them. There were more than a few tears as some recognised, for the first time, just how securely, yet gently, God had kept his loving hand on their lives.

If you are feeling your age right now, it might help you to look back over your life and recognise the faithfulness of God.

COLOSSIANS 3:1–4

Think about heaven

Since, then, you have been raised with Christ, set your hearts on things above, where Christ is seated at the right hand of God. Set your minds on things above, not on earthly things. For you died, and your life is now hidden with Christ in God. When Christ, who is your life, appears, then you also will appear with him in glory.

Heaven is *the* reality. Yet, even as Christians, we very often live forgetting that fact. In these verses, Paul says we have already been raised with Christ. Our new life has begun, but the best of it is hidden with Christ until we arrive 'home'.

The pain and discomfort, the mundane and messy experiences that we are going through right now are not what we were designed for. The best *is* yet to come. Part of our problem is that we fail to gain a heavenly perspective on this life. It is eternity that goes on for ever—not the life we're living now.

In New College Chapel, Oxford, there is a sculpture of Lazarus, just raised from the dead by Jesus. It shows him from the rear, as if from inside the tomb, looking back over his shoulder. His face reveals an almost unbearable sadness at leaving behind the paradise in heaven, in order to retake his place on earth. It says much about our inability to grasp the wonder of all that God has waiting for us.

But what is the relevance of heaven to the next medical test, the journey to the operating theatre, the bewildering words of our doctor, or the pain that never seems to ease?

Sometimes worry and pain take over and it's tough to look heavenward. What is now seems more real than what is 'for ever', but Paul urges us to set our minds on 'things above' because that's where the future is. That's *real* life.

God will help us to gain the heavenly perspective—if we just ask.

Friday

MARK 6:48–51

Inside out

[Jesus] saw the disciples straining at the oars, because the wind was against them. About the fourth watch of the night he went out to them, walking on the lake. He was about to pass by them, but when they saw him walking on the lake, they thought he was a ghost. They cried out, because they all saw him and were terrified. Immediately he spoke to them and said, 'Take courage! It is I. Don't be afraid.' Then he climbed into the boat with them, and the wind died down.

Even though the disciples have witnessed Jesus' miraculous feeding of a huge crowd (vv. 30–44), they are still unable to understand the providence of the Father and the power of his Son. Jesus is not very far away, and probably never intended to stay behind for long. Yet without his close presence these men become frightened and desperate.

The wind and waves are against them, and things are getting tough. Jesus sees what is happening from a distance. When his friends cry out, he 'immediately' (v. 50) responds, climbs into the boat and reassures them, bringing calm to the situation.

God often allows us to go ahead into a difficult situation seemingly without him. We may struggle for a while, even forget him in our efforts to control the situation ourselves, but he never takes his eyes off us.

Hilary McDowell, herself disabled and yet wonderfully enabled by God in ministry, writes, 'In my experience he fulfils his potential for our lives, not necessarily by removing the difficulties, but by climbing inside them with us and transforming them from within.'

There may be moments when you feel abandoned in your metaphorical wind and waves. Cry out and ask God to climb into your boat and transform things from within.

Weekend Two

Like a child

My heart is not proud, O Lord, my eyes are not haughty; I do not concern myself with great matters or things too wonderful for me. But I have stilled and quieted my soul; like a weaned child with its mother, like a weaned child is my soul within me. O Israel, put your hope in the Lord both now and for evermore.

This beautiful illustration of humility and dependence on God is a sight familiar to all of us: an infant who has learned that, close to its mother, it can rest secure. It can survey a puzzling world from this place of safety.

In the same way, the psalmist has learned that some things are too complex for his understanding. He is prepared to trust the all-seeing, all-knowing God with those 'great matters' (v. 1).

The child in these verses has known sustenance and comfort at its mother's breast. That past experience gives a reassurance that can be relied upon now and in the future. Likewise, God's parenting is as sure and certain today and tomorrow as it was yesterday.

While waiting for test results or diagnoses, we can be tempted to hypothesise, to leap forward into the 'Why?'s and 'What if?'s of life. But leaping when you are ill can be exhausting! We may need to learn the simple lesson of trust that this psalm teaches, accepting that while we may not have the answers, God does.

Stillness and quietness are not easy to find in a busy day or a hospital ward, but neither are children always held close in a peaceful place. We are more likely to see them taking refuge in this way when their surroundings are bewildering.

Our closeness to God offers us stillness and trust whatever our circumstances. We just have to climb into his lap.

MATTHEW 26:36–38

The comfort of friends

Then Jesus went with his disciples to a place called Gethsemane, and he said to them, 'Sit here while I go over there and pray.' He took Peter and the two sons of Zebedee along with him, and he began to be sorrowful and troubled. Then he said to them, 'My soul is overwhelmed with sorrow to the point of death. Stay here and keep watch with me.'

These verses are among the most touching in the Gospels, illustrating Jesus' humanity and his need for human comfort. It is easy to think that the Son's close relationship with the Father meant that he wouldn't need others in difficult times. But here he specifically asks for the company of close friends.

Once Jesus found himself in this close company, he was able to become vulnerable and show his grief. He knew that there wasn't much these friends could do but watch and pray—and they might even fail in that, but he was comforted to have them with him.

If Jesus sought the company of real friends in difficult times, how much more do we need to? It helps them, and us, if we can be specific about our needs. If more than half an hour at our bedside is tiring for us, we should gently say so. Chances are, it's just as tiring for them to be entertaining for so long!

When I was in hospital, one of my closest friends chose simply to sit with me quietly in the early morning hours. If she found me asleep, she would sit and pray silently before slipping away again. I was the recipient of a very special gift of her being there for me and 'keeping watch'.

Lord, send me those friends who will simply 'keep watch with me' (v. 38).

Tuesday

ISAIAH 40:29–31

Walking without fainting

He gives strength to the weary and increases the power of the weak. Even youths grow tired and weary, and young men stumble and fall; but those who hope in the Lord will renew their strength. They will soar on wings like eagles; they will run and not grow weary, they will walk and not be faint.

How much we depend on God! He is the source of our strength, physical and spiritual. He also knows that we will often try to run before we can walk. These verses remind us that if we are to avoid stumbling and falling, we must recognise that our strength and hope are in him, and that he will support us by his power. Once we acknowledge that, we will not just walk or run our way through the spiritual race he has set for us. We will soar effortlessly, like an eagle, which uses the surrounding air currents to great advantage, lifted by their supporting power.

Physical weakness is common to all of us, whatever our age. Illness and surgery often render even the strongest man as weak as a kitten. We are shocked by the shuffling walk which is all that we can manage. Our tendency to fall asleep, yet again, even after hours of slumber, bewilders us. Our frustration and impatience often become more of a handicap than the illness itself.

We forget that God has designed us to live at varying speeds. Our bodies bend so that we can sit, support us as we crawl, hold us upright to walk and eventually propel us to run. There may be times when we can't do any of those things, but there can still be moments when we soar higher than we ever believed possible—not on wings, but in the spirit.

Be patient. Physical healing and recovery take place at God's pace but spiritual strength is 'made perfect in weakness' (see 2 Corinthians 12:9–10).

2 CORINTHIANS 1:3–5

Special knowledge

Praise be to the God and Father of our Lord Jesus Christ, the Father of compassion and the God of all comfort, who comforts us in all our troubles, so that we can comfort those in any trouble with the comfort we ourselves have received from God. For just as the sufferings of Christ flow over into our lives, so also through Christ our comfort overflows.

If we have known something of the depths of suffering, we may be more able to offer something of the depths of compassion to others, but only if we have allowed our suffering to be transformed by God, letting him illuminate our darkness from within.

Paul suggests that when we have received God's comfort in our own pain, we are better able to empathise with others. That doesn't mean that God puts us through a tough time in order to turn us into some kind of martyr. It is something of a special training, though, because we are being given a unique potential for loving out of our own experience: 'For just as the sufferings of Christ flow over into our lives, so also through Christ our comfort overflows' (v. 5).

It is not the pain itself, but God's comfort in it, that transforms us—and it is that comfort, learnt through experience, that we pass on to others.

Many of us recognise that 'special something' which those who have known God's comfort in tough times often give to others. There is something in their approach that we can't quite put our finger on—a hidden wisdom and attitude of care.

The first step may be to allow ourselves to be on the receiving end of such compassion, knowing that one day that same comfort will overflow from Christ, through ourselves, to others.

There is no more effective healer than a healer who bears his own scars.

Thursday

LAMENTATIONS 3:25–26, 31–33

Compassion, hope and suffering

The Lord is good to those whose hope is in him, to the one who seeks him; it is good to wait quietly for the salvation of the Lord… For men are not cast off by the Lord for ever. Though he brings grief, he will show compassion, so great is his unfailing love. For he does not willingly bring affliction or grief to the children of men.

Sceptics say that grief is evidence of a God indifferent to human suffering. These verses say otherwise, by linking suffering and grief with God's goodness and the hope of salvation.

The Christian life is not sold with an insurance policy against suffering and grief. They are an inevitable—sometimes large—part of that life. But they are also part of a greater plan, hidden from our view. That's where hope comes in. Theologian Alister McGrath writes, 'Think of suffering as "the strange work of God". It is not an end in itself, but a means to a greater end—that of bringing us home to God, where suffering is transfigured and eventually defeated.'

'That's all very well!' we cry. 'But how does that help me now? Does God know how bad this is?' Hearing that God doesn't willingly put us through tough times, but often does so to bring us closer to him, may leave us feeling reluctant to share that closeness. But that's to miss the point of God's longing for relationship with us at all costs. God does allow—even bring—what he hates in order to achieve what he loves: our turning to him is what he longs for. He has endured pain and struggle too. His compassion and unfailing love shown in the life and death of Jesus witness to that fact. That can be a source of comfort—if we let it.

If we are quiet and still enough in the midst of struggle for him to hold us close, we will hear him whisper, 'I know, I know…'

Friday

ISAIAH 55:8–9

A different way of thinking

'For my thoughts are not your thoughts, neither are your ways my ways,' declares the Lord. 'As the heavens are higher than the earth, so are my ways higher than your ways and my thoughts than your thoughts.'

I am glad that God's thoughts and ways are higher than mine. Of course, acknowledging this can lead to a life filled with irresponsible resignation rather than hope-filled resolution. But to know God is to be free of the constant need to understand why, and how, and what he is doing in our lives, and simply to trust *him*—not our limited understanding of what befalls us.

God is long-sighted when we are short-sighted. He knows what lies behind the scenes when we are still tugging at the safety curtain. He is the composer of the whole symphony while we do little more than 'ping' a triangle—and usually out of time. He is God and we are sinful, self-centred men and women.

I'm a real fan of flying. When I am up in a plane, I just enjoy the flight. I do not need to understand the controls or ask the pilot how he will get me down again. Trusting in his authority, experience and skill, I get on with looking at the view.

So why do we so often question the way that God pilots our life? We are so headstrong and independent that when something like illness befalls us, we think we have to tell God exactly what he should do. We helpfully suggest what we should suffer and the date by which we should be well, and then bombard him with questions along the way. Isn't it better to trust him with the controls, hold our breath in the ups, hold him tight for the downs and enjoy the view in between?

'You will keep in perfect peace him whose mind is steadfast, because he trusts in you' (Isaiah 26:3).

PSALM 73:23–26

A source of true strength

Yet I am always with you; you hold me by my right hand. You guide me with your counsel, and afterward you will take me into glory. Whom have I in heaven but you? And earth has nothing I desire besides you. My flesh and my heart may fail, but God is the strength of my heart and my portion forever.

It has been said that Psalm 73 resembles the book of Job in a nutshell. These verses certainly mirror Job's final personal encounter with God as he reaches a reconciled relationship with his creator (Job 42). Even though many of his questions are left unanswered, in this world at least, Job, like the psalmist, comes to know that nothing else matters but God.

It's a trust which accepts that although we may be broken, covered with sores, ruined financially or mocked by neighbours, we can retain our spiritual strength. God holds us by the hand—for eternity.

It is understandable that we will cling to this life and make a healthy body a priority. We are reminded here to look beyond the stiffness, soreness and 'doesn't work as well as it used to' aspect of our physical lives to the spiritual strength we should ask for, which will fit us well not just for this life but ultimately for heaven. God himself can be our strength. He is all we need.

Notice the emphasis here, though. It is up to us to stay with him, to allow him to hold us by the hand. Only when we are walking in step with him, hands clasped, is he able to guide us, give us his counsel and afterwards take us to be with him in glory.

Reflect on the way you or those around you walk together and gain strength from each other in different ways. Is your walk with God mirrored?

PSALM 22:1, 3–5

Forsaken? Yet...

My God, my God, why have you forsaken me? Why are you so far from saving me, so far from the words of my groaning? ... Yet you are enthroned as the Holy One... In you our fathers put their trust... They cried to you and were saved; in you they trusted and were not disappointed.

This heart-wrenching psalm is a piercing cry born out of painful experience. The experience of the psalmist merges with that of Jesus in those moments of agony and isolation on the cross.

When we claim these words as our own, we share, in some small way, a 'fellowship of suffering' (see Philippians 3:10) with Jesus. We identify with him when we feel abandoned by God but paradoxically know that we have nowhere else to go but to him.

A flicker of faith shines in that qualifying 'Yet' (v. 3). Even with a desperate cry, God is acknowledged. His sovereignty and trustworthiness are remembered, almost as an act of will. 'It is in the moment of desolation that the sufferer binds himself fastly to God... God was still "my God"' (James Jones).

When we experience a feeling of abandonment, trust can sometimes be an act of want followed by an act of will. That's enough for God. Our trust may resemble only hanging on to him by our fingertips, but God's response, sooner or later, is to remind us that he has been hanging on to us much more securely.

Our greatest practical need at these times is for someone who can share our pain—and our tears—honestly, without platitudes and 'one size fits all' Bible verses. We need someone who will go the long haul, weep with us and remind us gently that this time will pass and that they will stay with us until it does.

Father, send me someone to share the darkness, and help us to find you hidden there.

Tuesday

ISAIAH 40:10–11

Looking after the young

See, the Sovereign Lord comes with power, and his arm rules for him. See, his reward is with him, and his recompense accompanies him. He tends his flock like a shepherd: he gathers the lambs in his arms and carries them close to his heart; he gently leads those that have young.

These words paint a contrasting picture of our God. He rules with power and authority, but loves us with tenderness and care.

We are assured that the Lord, the shepherd-king, carries the very young of his flock close to his heart, held tightly in his arms, and that he gently leads their parents.

It is a vivid picture, full of reassurance that God cares for families—especially, perhaps, those families who become temporarily separated because of the illness or weakness of one family member, and who need his special care.

Leaving children at home to spend time in hospital can be heart-breaking. Suddenly we are removed from all the tender domestic details that make up family life. We miss bedtimes and birthdays, loving and laughter. Separation hurts! Their visits to us in hospital can be tense or stressful. Older children may have endless questions which we can't answer, and it's hard not to worry about how everyone will cope as they leave our side.

Some of us may even need to contemplate the prospect of leaving our children as we face death. I believe there is no pain like it. It is at these moments that we need to remember that in the midst of such uncertainty, God *is* certain.

God's parenting of us, and of our families, can be trusted. We need to hand over our children and wider family—often repeatedly—into the loving arms of the shepherd, who will carry them close to his heart as he leads us forward.

ROMANS 8:26–27

How to pray when you're weak

The Spirit helps us in our weakness. We do not know what we ought to pray for,
but the Spirit himself intercedes for us with groans that words cannot express.
And he who searches our hearts knows the mind of the Spirit, because the Spirit
intercedes for the saints in accordance with God's will.

We cannot do without the Holy Spirit. We pray to the Father, through the Son, and with the Holy Spirit. Our need of him is never greater than when we are weak and just don't know how or what to pray. Sometimes, prayers from the depths of our hearts cannot be put into words. We don't know what God's will is, but the Spirit does. He articulates the cry of our hearts for us, in 'sighs too deep for words' (v. 26, RSV) and 'in accordance with God's will' (v. 27, NIV).

We don't have to fret when words and prayers fail us. The Father searches our uplifted hearts and the Holy Spirit joins that search to express what he finds. That's why our weakness—physical, emotional or spiritual— is made strong through prayer.

Often words cannot express how we feel. So how do we use Paul's promise of the Holy Spirit's help in practical ways? Perhaps by using those forms of communication that come more easily, and by allowing the Spirit to do the rest.

Writing, talking with others, quietly reflecting, taking a walk in beautiful countryside (even if just in our imagination) and listening to music can all lift our hearts to God, enabling the Holy Spirit to help us. When I was at my very lowest point in hospital I found it helpful to listen to music. Samuel Barber's *Adagio for Strings* perfectly expressed the physical and emotional pain I was feeling. Through its yearning strains, I found that my heart somehow met the heart of God the Father.

Prayers prayed when we're weak are not weak prayers.

HABAKKUK 3:17–18

Yet I will rejoice in the Lord

Though the fig-tree does not bud and there are no grapes on the vines, though the olive crop fails and the fields produce no food, though there are no sheep in the pen and no cattle in the stalls, yet I will rejoice in the Lord, I will be joyful in God my Saviour.

Habakkuk has wrestled with his maker but here he has come to realise that God's ways are perfect, whatever the circumstances. He has learnt that God is big enough to take his anger, that gut-wrenching questions are honouring to God because they come from a vulnerable heart which recognises the need for the Almighty to answer. At these times, God himself becomes more important than our faith. As we cling to him, even if our grip is weak, we will sow a seed of joy that enables us to rejoice in the one who is immeasurably greater than our pain.

As I write, today is the fifth anniversary of my cancer diagnosis, and I can truly celebrate all that God has meant to me over those years. On that difficult day five years ago, my Bible reading contained these very verses. It is a complete 'God-incidence' that I am writing about them today: that's the kind of thing God does!

In my diary entry that day, I wrote the verses out in full to remind myself that whatever diagnosis I was given, I could still rejoice in the Lord. He was still the God of my salvation. In the evening I wrote, 'It's definitely cancer. Yet I will rejoice in the Lord.'

Those words weren't a glib attempt at superspirituality. They were my honest response after four weeks of tests and pain, prayer and uncertainty.

Oswald Chambers said, 'Faith never knows where it is being led, but it loves and knows the one who is leading.'

Friday

REVELATION 21:3–4

All things will pass

And I heard a loud voice from the throne saying, 'Now the dwelling of God is with men, and he will live with them. They will be his people, and God himself will be with them and be their God. He will wipe every tear from their eyes. There will be no more death or mourning or crying or pain, for the old order of things has passed away.'

One day, we are told, all this will be over. There will be no more pain or death. Both will do more than pale into insignificance, they will be 'no more' (v. 4). We will be with God himself, living a new, wonderful, pain-free life that will never again be scattered with tears, numbed through grief or scarred by agony.

This is the heavenly perspective that we are urged to retain throughout our life on earth, the sure and certain knowledge that all things will pass and our suffering will be transformed by the light and love of an eternity spent with the Father.

One of the most common longings among those in hospital is the longing to go home. There is nothing like the familiarity of our own space, our own bed, and the faces of those we love. We look forward to all the things we will do 'when we get home' and feel sure that we will feel so much better. Often the reality is a little different. Going home can be more tiring than we imagined, even stressful. We lose the knowledge and availability of the medical staff and are left to our own devices.

Going to heaven won't be like that, because we are going home to God himself. He will welcome us, live among us and banish fear, doubt, worry and sadness. Do you know what it is like to have someone wipe away tears from your eyes? God himself will do it!

Let that certain hope of a welcome home—on earth and heaven—draw you to worship.

Weekend Four

PSALM 16:8–11

Resting secure

I have set the Lord always before me. Because he is at my right hand, I will not be shaken. Therefore my heart is glad and my tongue rejoices; my body will also rest secure, because you will not abandon me to the grave, nor will you let your Holy One see decay. You have made known to me the path of life; you will fill me with joy in your presence, with eternal pleasures at your right hand.

This psalm communicates something of David's personal relation-ship with God at a time when his life is uncertain. He knows that it is God who has set him on his current path—however difficult it may be—so he will remain secure whatever happens. Because the Lord is nearby, David will 'not be shaken' (v. 8).

That assurance produces gladness, praise and rest in David's life, and growing confidence that whatever happens, even death is not the end. Rather, it is the beginning of joy in the presence of the one who has been with David all his life.

How can we know such assurance at a time when health, even life, is uncertain? David's trusting relationship was based on his experience of God's faithfulness. That experience builds confidence for the future.

Secondly, the Lord is David's focus. We should remind ourselves that he is with us at our 'right hand', and that fixing our eyes on him can keep us on firm ground (v. 8).

Next, God's raising of his Son reminds us that whatever happens to us in death, we will be with him beyond it.

Lastly, David's 'therefore' (v. 9) exudes a confidence that can be ours too.

In quiet moments today, practise 'resting secure' in the presence of God.

Our Bible reading notes

BRF offers five different series of Bible reading notes which approach the Bible in different ways to help you enjoy reading and begin to understand the Bible's message. Which one is best for you?

New Daylight is our most popular series. The full Bible text is included. The passage is explained by one of our experienced writers, who will help readers understand the Bible passage and how it is relevant for their own spiritual journey. Available in print, Deluxe edition (includes larger print size), app for Android, iPhone and iPad and daily email.

Guidelines is for people who are hungry for a deeper study, who are ready to hear what current biblical scholarship has to say, what differing theological viewpoints may exist, and who want to make up their own mind on how the passage becomes relevant for them. Available in print, app for Android, iPhone and iPad and PDF.

You can find out more from

- your local Christian bookshop
- www.biblereadingnotes.org.uk
- BRF Direct 01865 319700

Day by Day with God provides a woman's eyes' view on the Bible. Written by women for women with an evangelical emphasis, taking account of the things that matter most to women. Available in print and app for Android, iPhone and iPad.

The Upper Room contains meditations that show real people living faithfully in real-life situations, with the Bible as the touchstone for and measure of faithful living. The meditations are provided by *The Upper Room* readers themselves from around the world. Ideal for new Christians. Available in print and PDF.

Quiet Spaces is for people who enjoy exploring the Bible using their innate spirituality and creativity. Each edition contains nine themes explored in different ways. These include biblical reflections, views on the theme from a wide sweep of Christian tradition and history, prayers and meditations and a creative activity to take the reader deeper into the theme. Available in print.

Available the way you want to read!

BRF Bible reading notes are available in a printed booklet, as an app for Android, iPhone or iPad, or as a PDF download for your laptop or PC, meaning your notes are easily available whenever that spare five minutes appears in your day!

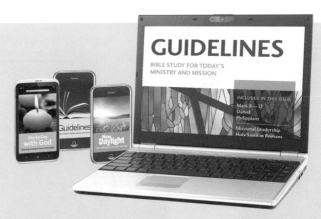

Bridget & Adrian Plass

The Apple of His Eye

Discovering God's loving purpose for each one of us

Bridget Plass

First published in 1996, Bridget explores the Bible passages which tell of God's loving purpose for each one of us, as well as for our wider communities.

pb, 978 1 84101 088 5, 160 pages, £7.99
Available for Kindle

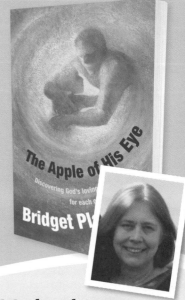

The Unlocking

God's escape plan for frightened people

Adrian Plass

The Unlocking is a book that has established itself as a Christian classic. Adrian takes you on a voyage of discovery through the Bible, exploring fearful situations—and frightened people—and reflecting on some of the many ways in which God meets you with his healing love and grace, no matter how daunting your circumstances.

pb, 978 0 7459 3510 2, 160 pages, £7.99
Available for Kindle